SHAKESPEARE'S ROMEO AND JULIET

AN AQA ESSAY WRITING GUIDE

R. P. DAVIS

For Leah.

CONTENTS

FOREWORD

In your GCSE English Literature exam, you will be presented with an extract from Shakespeare's *Romeo and Juliet* and a question that asks you to offer both a close analysis of the extract plus a commentary of the play as a whole. Of course, there are many methods one *might* use to tackle this style of question. However, there is one particular technique which, due to its sophistication, most readily allows students to unlock the highest marks: namely, **the thematic method**.

To be clear, this study guide is *not* intended to walk you through the play scene-by-scene: there are many great guides out there that do just that. No, this guide, by sifting through a series of mock exam questions, will demonstrate *how* to organise a response thematically and thus write a stellar essay: a skill we believe no other study guide adequately covers!

I have encountered students who have structured their essays all sorts of ways: some by writing about the extract line by line, others by identifying various language techniques and giving each its own paragraph. The method I'm advocating, on the other hand, involves picking out three to four themes that will allow you to holistically answer the question: these three to four themes will become the three to four content paragraphs of your essay, cushioned between a brief introduction and conclusion. Ideally, these themes will follow from one to the next to create a flowing argument. Within each of these thematic paragraphs, you can then ensure you are jumping through the mark scheme's hoops.

So to break things down further, each thematic paragraph will include various point-scoring components. In each paragraph, you will quote from the extract, offer analyses of these quotes, then discuss how the specific language techniques you have identified illustrate the theme you're discussing. In each paragraph, you will also discuss how other parts of the play further illustrate the theme (or even complicate it). And in each, you will comment on the era in which the play was written and how that helps to understand the chosen theme.

Don't worry if this all feels daunting. Throughout this guide, I will be illustrating in great detail – by means of examples – how to build an essay of this kind.

The beauty of the thematic approach is that, once you have your themes, you suddenly have a direction and a trajectory, and this makes essay writing a whole lot easier. However, it must also be noted that extracting themes in

The Shakespearian equivalent of a selfie.

the first place is something students often find tricky. I have come across many candidates who understand the extract and the play inside out; but when they are presented with a question under exam conditions, and the pressure kicks in, they find it tough to break their response down into themes. The fact of the matter is: the process is a *creative* one and the best themes require a bit of imagination.

In this guide, I shall take seven different exam-style questions, coupled with extracts from the play, and put together a plan for each – a plan that illustrates in detail how we will be satisfying the mark scheme's criteria. Please do keep in mind that, when operating under timed conditions, your plans will necessarily be less detailed than those that appear in this volume.

Now, you might be asking whether three or four themes is best. The truth is, you should do whatever you feel most comfortable with: the examiner is looking for an original, creative answer, and not sitting there counting the themes. So if you think you are quick enough to cover four, then great. However, if you would rather do three to make sure you do each theme justice, that's also fine. I sometimes suggest that my student pick four themes, but make the fourth one smaller – sort of like an afterthought, or an observation that turns things on their head. That way, if they feel they won't have time to explore this fourth theme in its own right, they can always give it a quick mention in the conclusion instead.

The Globe Theatre in London. It was built on the site of the original, which was burnt down in 1613.

Before I move forward in earnest, I believe it to be worthwhile to run through the four Assessment Objectives the exam board want you to cover in your response – if only to demonstrate how effective the thematic response can be. I would argue that the first Assessment Objective (AO1) – the one that wants candidates to 'read, understand and respond to texts' and which is worth 12 of the total 34 marks up for grabs – will be wholly satisfied by selecting strong themes, then fleshing them out with quotes. Indeed, when it comes to identifying the top-scoring candidates for AO1, the mark scheme explicitly tells examiners to look for a 'critical, exploratory, conceptualised response' that makes 'judicious use of precise references' – the word 'concept' is a synonym of theme, and 'judicious references' simply refers to quotes that appropriately support the theme you've chosen.

The second Assessment Objective (AO2) – which is also responsible for 12 marks – asks students to 'analyse the language, form and structure used by a writer to create meanings and effects, using relevant subject terminology where appropriate.' As noted, you will already be quoting from the play as you back up your themes, and it is a natural progression to then analyse the language techniques used. In fact, this is far more effective than simply observing language techniques (personification here, alliteration there), because by discussing how the language techniques relates to and shapes the theme, you will also be demonstrating how the writer 'create[s] meanings and effects.'

Now, in my experience, language analysis is the most important element of AO2 – perhaps 8 of the 12 marks will go towards language analysis. You will also notice, however, that AO2 asks students to comment on 'form and structure.' Again, the thematic approach has your back – because though simply jamming in a point on form or structure will feel jarring, when you bring these points up while discussing a theme, as a means to further a thematic argument, you will again organically be discussing the way it 'create[s] meanings and effects.'

AO3 requires you to 'show understanding of the relationships between texts and the contexts in which they were written' and is responsible for a more modest 6 marks in total. These are easy enough to weave into a thematic argument; indeed, the theme gives the student a chance to bring up context in a relevant and fitting way. After all, you don't want it to look like you've just shoehorned a contextual factoid into the mix.

| The Globe Theatre's interior.

My hope is that this book, by demonstrating how to tease out themes from an extract, will help you feel more confident in doing so yourself. I believe it is also worth mentioning that the themes I have picked out are by no means definitive. Asked the very same question, someone else may pick out different themes, and write an answer that is just as good (if not better!). Obviously the exam is not likely to be fun – my memory of them is pretty much the exact opposite. But still, this is one of the very few chances that you will get at GCSE level to actually be creative. And to my mind at least, that was always more enjoyable – if *enjoyable* is the right word – than simply demonstrating that I had memorised loads of facts.

ESSAY PLAN ONE

READ THE FOLLOWING EXTRACT FROM
ACT 1 SCENE 2 OF ROMEO AND JULIET
AND THEN ANSWER THE QUESTION THAT
FOLLOWS.

At this point in the play, Paris is asking Capulet for Juliet's hand in marriage.

PARIS

But now, my lord, what say you to my suit?

CAPULET

But saying o'er what I have said before:
My child is yet a stranger in the world;
She hath not seen the change of fourteen years,
Let two more summers wither in their pride,
Ere we may think her ripe to be a bride.

PARIS

Younger than she are happy mothers made.

CAPULET

And too soon marr'd are those so early made.
The earth hath swallow'd all my hopes but she,
She is the hopeful lady of my earth:
But woo her, gentle Paris, get her heart,
My will to her consent is but a part;

An she agree, within her scope of choice
Lies my consent and fair according voice.

Starting with this extract, explore the degree to which you think Shakespeare portrays Lord Capulet as a bad father.

Write about:

• **how Shakespeare portrays Capulet in this extract.**

• **how Shakespeare portrays Capulet in the play as a whole.**

Introduction

The introduction should be short and sweet, yet still pack a punch. I personally like to score an early context point (AO3) in the opening sentence. Then, in the second sentence, I like to hint at the themes I'm going to cover, so that the examiner feels as though they have their bearings and is thus ready to hand out AO1 marks.

In this instance, I score early AO3 marks by invoking another Shakespeare text that places *Romeo and Juliet* in context. After this, I keep things short and sweet, hinting at the ambivalent approach I am about to take.[1]

"Father-daughter relationships abound in Shakespeare: the other mid-1590s sister play to *Romeo and Juliet* – *A Midsummer's Night Dream* – starts with a father,

Egeus, threatening his daughter, Hermia, with unwanted wedlock. However, while Capulet puts on a similar performance, he also embodies a host of admirable qualities that complicate an audience's perception."

Theme/Paragraph One: Capulet exhibits genuine concern for his daughter's wellbeing: in this extract, he is particularly concerned about his daughter marrying too young. However, this is undercut later in the play by his heavy-handed attempt at discipline.

- As suitors go, Paris is hardly presented as a menacing presence: he politely asks Capulet for Juliet's hand: 'what say you of my suit?' Nevertheless, Capulet quickly makes known his worries about Juliet's extreme youth ('not seen the change of fourteen years'), and exhibits concern that an early marriage could be detrimental: 'Too soon marr'd are those early made.' The alliteration of 'marr'd' and 'made' adds emphasis to Capulet's point by powerfully linking these words: those who get made in marriage too soon end up marred.[2] Capulet seems genuinely concerned for his daughter's wellbeing and the implication of her tender age. [*AO1 for advancing the argument with a judiciously selected quote; AO2 for the close analysis of the language*].

- However, although Capulet is presented as a caring father towards Juliet here, elsewhere he is presented as the polar opposite. In Act 3 Scene 5, Capulet, in the wake of Juliet's refusal to marry Paris, threatens his daughter with violence ('my fingers itch') and brutally objectifies her: 'You be mine, I'll give you to my friend.'

Theme/Paragraph Two: Capulet in this extract is portrayed as emotionally frail, and arguably this frailty leads to an anxiety-driven, rash decision.

- Capulet in this extract is oddly mercurial and rash in his decision making: at first, he is against Paris courting his daughter; yet, in the space of a few lines, he changes his mind: 'woo her gentle Paris.'[3]
- Although it might be argued that this vacillation should be attributed to Capulet's deep concern for his daughter – an instinct to marry her to someone who can provide for her – on closer inspection, this is only half the story. Capulet lets slip that he has lost other offspring: he claims that 'The earth hath swallow'd all my hopes but she' – the image of a personified earth eating his hopes communicating the fact other offspring have been buried, while the elision in 'swallow'd' has the missing 'e' mirror this loss.[4] As a result of this emotional wound, Capulet goes against his own better judgement to 'let two more summers wither' and makes a rash *volte-face*.[5] His concern for his daughter, therefore, is not only counterbalanced by a fierce temper, but also compromised by an emotional wound that muddles Capulet's decision making. [*AO1 for advancing the argument with a judiciously selected quote; AO2 for the close analysis of the language*].
- However, later in the play, one sees that Capulet's

frailty lends him greater emotional intelligence as a father: after Juliet feigns her death in Act 4, Capulet mourns her death with moving poetry: 'Death lies on her like an untimely frost / Upon the sweetest flower.' That this elegy comes right at the close of Act 4 lends it extra structural emphasis, since the natural pause between acts forces the audience to linger on the words.[6] [*AO2 for observing how structure shapes meaning*].

Theme/Paragraph Three. Capulet is a good father insofar as he sets a positive example in the way he interacts with the wider world.

- In this passage, Capulet comes across as a positive role model in the community. He deals with Paris in a calm, respectful manner – even though Paris is pursuing his young daughter. Even if one disagrees with his final response, he does show *patience* with Paris. Indeed, Capulet does not monologue at Paris; rather, there is a respectful back and forth, and Capulet gives Paris space to speak. This is exemplified by Paris's line – 'younger than she are happy mothers made' – midway through the extract: Shakespeare, by interpolating this line amid Capulet's words, uses form to relay a sense of respectful dialogue. [*AO2 for observing how form shapes meaning*].
- *Elsewhere in the play*: At Capulet's party, Capulet attempts to keep the peace when Tybalt is trying to escalate tensions with the Montague gatecrashers. However, whereas Capulet cast himself as a respectable role model in this scene, at other points in the play he falls well short: the audience's very first

introduction to Capulet, prior to this extract, sees him seeming to lust for violence: 'Give me my long sword, ho!' – Shakespeare's structural decision to place this line in the play's opening scene lending it extra emphasis. [*AO2 for observing how structure shapes meaning*].

Conclusion

I have a smaller theme tucked up my sleeve; however, given the length of the previous themes, it feels wisest to integrate it into the conclusion. I wish to point out that Capulet exhibits a flexibility that boosts our estimation of his fathering abilities...

"Capulet – like the play in which he appears – embodies powerful contrasts: he is a positive role model to Juliet, yet a provocateur; an empathetic father, but callous.[7] This extract exemplifies Shakespeare's flair for ambiguity. Although one might argue (as above) that Capulet's volte-face ought to be considered a flaw, it could equally be considered a virtue: he has an admirable capacity for flexibility, which allows him to hew to Juliet's choices in a way that empowers her: 'Within her scope of choice / Lies my consent and fair according voice.' The audience is left feeling as if Capulet is 'a stranger in this world' – an individual beyond our ability to definitively decipher."

The Shakespeare and Company bookstore in Paris (the city, not the man!)

READ THE FOLLOWING EXTRACT FROM
ACT 1 SCENE 5 OF ROMEO AND JULIET
AND THEN ANSWER THE QUESTION THAT
FOLLOWS.

At this point in the play, Romeo has gate-crashed the Capulet's party and has set eyes on Juliet for the first time

ROMEO

[To a Servingman] What lady is that, which doth
enrich the hand
Of yonder knight?

SERVANT

I know not, sir.

ROMEO

O, she doth teach the torches to burn bright!
It seems she hangs upon the cheek of night
Like a rich jewel in an Ethiope's ear;
Beauty too rich for use, for earth too dear!
So shows a snowy dove trooping with crows,
As yonder lady o'er her fellows shows.
The measure done, I'll watch her place of stand,
And, touching hers, make blessed my rude hand.

Did my heart love till now? forswear it, sight!
For I ne'er saw true beauty till this night.

Starting with this dialogue, explain how Shakespeare presents Romeo's feelings towards Juliet.

Write about:

• **how Shakespeare presents Romeo's feelings towards Juliet in this extract.**

• **how Shakespeare presents Romeo's feelings towards Juliet in the play as a whole.**

Introduction

Again, I want to keep the introduction short and sweet. Again, I want to score some early AO3 marks:

"In this extract, Romeo – engaging in a tradition derived from Medieval courtly verse – enumerates the traits of his romantic-interest-to-be: Juliet. Romeo here, on first setting eyes on Juliet, exhibits not only astonishment, but also a lovesickness that is a hallmark of the courtly-love tradition. However, Romeo also objectifies and dehumanises Juliet in a way that foreshadows behaviour later in the play."

Theme/Paragraph One: Shakespeare portrays Romeo's feelings for Juliet as so intense that they induce both pleasure and pain at once: a kind of paradoxical lovesickness.

- Packed within Romeo's statement that Juliet manifests 'beauty too rich for use, for earth too dear' is the insinuation that he finds the sight of Juliet *painfully overwhelming*: her beauty is so great, so excessive, that it not only defies comprehension, but also seems to be too much for the earth to accommodate: 'for earth too dear.' That 'too dear' completes a rhyming couplet places emphasis on the excess it implies. [*AO1 for advancing the argument with a judiciously selected quote; AO2 for the close analysis of the language*].

- The staccato nature of Romeo's speech – the peppering of exclamation marks; the caesura; the abrupt self-questioning, voiced with three inverted trochaic feet ('Did my heart love till now?') – further reveals the extent of Romeo's lovesickness.[1] The overwhelming nature of Juliet's beauty, and the lovesickness it has induced, has knocked his mind painfully off-kilter. [*AO2 for the close analysis of the language*].

- By borrowing from the Medieval trope of courtly love-sickness, Shakespeare could be sincerely implying that Romeo's affection for Juliet transcends the here and now: it belongs to a tradition that massively predates Verona's 'piteous overthrows.' [*AO3 for placing the text in a literary-historical context*].

- *Elsewhere in the play*: When Romeo asks 'Did my

heart love till now,' he also invites the audience to compare his reaction to Juliet to his prior reaction to Rosaline. When describing his affection for Rosaline, he similarly tried to impart a sense of overwhelming lovesickness, a sense that love was causing him agony. However, on that occasion, it came across as false and unnatural: 'O Brawling love, O loving hate, / O anything, of nothing first create!'

Theme/Paragraph Two: Romeo conceives of Juliet's beauty as transcendental – it surpasses any earthly phenomena he has hitherto encountered – and, as a result, he is struck by a sense of astonishment.

- When Romeo exclaims that 'O, she doth teach the torches to burn bright!,' he neatly captures the way in which Juliet's beauty breaks the mould: Juliet's beauty does not simply stand out ('burn bright') in a way reminiscent of a torch, but it *outdoes* the torches. Romeo posits a metaphor for beauty – the light of a torch – only to suggest that the metaphor does not suffice: Juliet is *more* beautiful than a torch is bright. [*AO1 for advancing the argument with a judiciously selected quote*].
- The image of a bright light is frequently deployed in literature not only to symbolise beauty, but also astonishment: Juliet brings to mind torches precisely because Romeo is experiencing such intense astonishment.
- *Elsewhere in the play*: Interestingly, the light motif appears throughout the play: in Act 2, Scene 2, for

instance, Romeo exclaims that 'The brightness of [Juliet's] cheek would shame those stars / As daylight doth a lamp.' Again, Romeo is using language of bright lights to both articulate Juliet's transcendental beauty and communicate his astonishment. [*AO1 for advancing the argument with a judiciously selected quote*].

- There are also language techniques throughout this passage that communicate Romeo's astonishment: the exclamation 'O' hints that Juliet's beauty has momentarily rendered Romeo speechless; moreover, the elision throughout the extract ('o'er' and 'ne'er') suggests the words are tumbling out of him at speeds that thwart vocalisation, but also tightens the verse's form, thereby keeping it taut, punchy, and more likely to have the audience also to exclaim, 'O.' The phraseology is reminiscent of the transcendental awe in the prologue to Shakespeare's *Henry V*, which also plays on light imagery: 'O for a muse of fire.' [*AO2 for the close analysis of the language; AO2 for observing how form shapes meaning; AO3 for bringing in another text that helps us understand the play in the wider cultural milieu*].

Theme/Paragraph Three: While Romeo's language seeks to cast Juliet as a transcendental entity, Shakespeare hints that Romeo's portrayal of Juliet is naive: Romeo is putting Juliet on an unrealistic pedestal, and setting expectations no mortal could satisfy.

- The way Romeo perceives Juliet frequently comes

across as startlingly naive. Perhaps the most
astounding attribute he projects onto Juliet is his
conviction that Juliet has a divine capacity to heal and
bless. Indeed, twice in this passage he hints that the
mere touch of Juliet's hand is enough to deliver divine
transcendence: 'which doth enrich the hand / Of
Yonder knight'; 'touching hers, make blessed my rude
hand.' Romeo, with all the zeal of an unworldly youth,
is naively projecting onto Juliet messianic healing
qualities. [*AO1 for advancing the argument with a
judiciously selected quote*].

- 'Yonder knight' is a loaded phrase: the word 'Knight'
  again naively elevates Juliet, since it implicitly casts
  her as the medieval maiden of the courtly tradition for
  whom knights would fight and die.

- *Elsewhere in the play*: Romeo demonstrates naivety
  not only in the ways he perceives Juliet, but also in his
  cavalier attitude towards the consequences of
  pursuing a marriage with Juliet: after all, the
  relationship can clearly not last given the animosity
  between their families.

**Theme/Paragraph Four: Shakespeare also draws
attention to the troubling, sexist ways Romeo
constructs Juliet: he sees her as an object that he
might possess and dehumanises her with animalistic imagery.**

- Romeo's comment that Juliet is 'too rich for use' is
  telling, since 'use' implies that she is an object that can
  be owned and, indeed, *used*. This follows a pattern
  throughout the play in which Romeo conceives of

Juliet as an object: in Act 2 Scene 6, just before they are due to marry, he states that 'it is enough I may but call her mine' – and, indeed, the word 'mine' is repeated again later in the scene. [*AO1 for advancing the argument with a judiciously selected quote*].

- It is also interesting that in this extract, Romeo discusses women in animalistic terms: he describes Juliet as a 'snowy dove,' whereas the other women he conceives of as 'crows.' Although this is intended as a compliment, it still functions to dehumanise Juliet. This may remind us of Capulet later comparing Juliet to 'a green-sickness carrion' – a piece of meat – thereby creating an implicit symmetry between Romeo and Capulet.

Conclusion

In this plan, I have elaborated on all the themes I wished to cover. As a result, my aim with the conclusion is simply to summarise:

"Although the focus of this passage is apparently on Juliet, Shakespeare reveals just as much about Romeo himself: his status as neo-courtly lover, his regressive attitude towards women, his capacity for astonishment. However, it is Romeo's naivety towards Juliet that is ultimately most striking. There is an awful irony in Romeo's attempt to foist on Juliet Christ-like healing qualities: his romantic contact with Juliet, after all, winds up the very locus of his destruction."

ESSAY PLAN THREE

READ THE FOLLOWING EXTRACT FROM
ACT 2 SCENE 3 OF ROMEO AND JULIET
AND THEN ANSWER THE QUESTION THAT
FOLLOWS.

A t this point in the play, Romeo has fallen in
love with Juliet and is seeking counsel from
the Friar.

ROMEO

I pray thee, chide not; she whom I love now
Doth grace for grace and love for love allow;
The other did not so.

FRIAR LAURENCE

O, she knew well
Thy love did read by rote and could not spell.
But come, young waverer, come, go with me,
In one respect I'll thy assistant be;
For this alliance may so happy prove,
To turn your households' rancour to pure love.

ROMEO

O, let us hence; I stand on sudden haste.

FRIAR LAURENCE

Wisely and slow; they stumble that run fast.

Starting with this conversation, explain how far you think Shakespeare presents the Friar as a positive influence?

Write about:

• how Shakespeare presents the Friar in this extract

• how Shakespeare presents the Friar in the play as a whole

Introduction

The introduction should be short and sweet, yet still pack a punch. I personally like to score an early context point (AO3) in the opening sentence. Then, in the second sentence, I like to quickly outline the themes I'm going to cover, so that the examiner feels as though they have their bearings and is thus ready to hand out AO1 marks.

"While Elizabethan England was a profoundly religious domain in which didactic instruction was paramount, it was also a deeply Protestant nation, paranoid of Catholicism's supposed malign influence.[1] Shakespeare's Catholic Friar captures this paradox: at once a moral guardian seeking to heal a feud and assist in Romeo's education, yet also a flawed hypocrite, acting against his own advice."

Theme/Paragraph One: The Friar, by taking measures to heal the feud between the Montagues and Capulets, functions as a positive, reconciliatory figure in the play.

- The Friar explicitly states his conciliatory objective: he wishes 'to turn [their] households' rancour to pure love.' The Friar is carefully invoking two juxtaposing concepts – 'rancour' and 'pure love' – and stating his desire to tame the former and alchemically convert it into the latter. Indeed, this taming process is reflected in the metre: whereas 'rancour' is a jarring, trochaic word, the phrase 'pure love' is a satisfying spondee. [*AO1 for advancing the argument with a judiciously selected quote; AO2 for the close analysis of the language*].

- The way the Friar pluralises the word household, and places a plural possessive apostrophe after it, emphasises the commonality between the Capulets and Montagues: he is drawing attention to what they have in common, not what separates them. [*AO2 for the close analysis of the language used*].

- The simplicity of the phrase 'pure love' shows the Friar's awareness that the love between Romeo and Juliet, which he wishes to spread more widely between the feuding families, is the real deal: this is not the phony, overblown 'brawling love' that Romeo had vocalised towards Rosaline.

- *Elsewhere in the play*: Arguably, the Friar's plan to heal the feud via the lovers *does* work: in the final scene, there appears to be a détente between the families. However, not only is this truce awkward (hardly 'pure love'), but it comes at a tremendous cost: the lovers, and many others, are dead. The Prince's remark – 'A glooming peace this morning with it brings' – captures the tension: the peace is marred by gloom. It might be noted that this comment arrives in the play's final speech: as a result of this structural choice, the audience is forced to linger uncomfortably on the unsatisfying outcome. [*AO1 for advancing the argument with a judiciously selected quote; AO2 for observing how structure shapes meaning*].

Theme/Paragraph Two: The friar is a fatherly figure to Romeo: he is an honest presence, who uses humour to enable Romeo to achieve greater self awareness.

- When the Friar asserts that 'Thy love did read by rote and could not spell,' he is teasing Romeo about the nature of his love for Rosaline: he is portraying it as a manufactured imitation of courtly love that Romeo has learned 'by rote.' Not only is he describing it as memorised rather than coming from his heart, but 'rote' is also a homophone of 'wrote' – which hints at the fact it was an artistic performance rather than the real deal. [*AO1 for advancing the argument with a judiciously selected quote; AO2 for the close analysis of the language*].

- The Friar also appears to use a nickname – 'Young waverer' – to tease Romeo for his mercuriality. The Friar is deploying gentle mockery to help Romeo achieve greater self awareness. Indeed, the Friar deploys this tactic even prior to the start of this extract, and it does appear to be yielding results: Romeo's opening lines in this passage demonstrates that he now understands that his love for Rosaline was never truly substantial: she did not return his 'grace for grace.' This theme of benevolent mockery is a favourite of Shakespeare's: in his 17th Century play, *King Lear*, the Fool repeatedly mocks Lear and, in so doing, helps him achieve self-awareness. [*AO1 for advancing the argument with a judiciously selected quote; AO3 for bringing in another text that helps us understand the play in the wider cultural milieu*].

- *Elsewhere in the play*: At other points in the play, the Friar again comes across as fatherly when he attempts to calm Romeo and Juliet down. This shows a different fatherly dimension: he is deescalating emotions and offering a release valve.

Theme/Paragraph Three: Although he seems to offer wise advice, he is directly – and damagingly – going against his own words (he fails to practice what he preaches!).

- While in this extract the Friar imparts seemingly ironclad advice to the hasty Romeo – 'Wisely and slow; they stumble that run fast' – the Friar directly contradicts himself by agreeing to marry the newly acquainted lovers. Certainly, the way the line is presented on the page – as part of a quick back-and-forth with Romeo, a literal one-liner – has the form mimic the 'sudden haste' of the Friar's actions. Indeed, it may not be lost on the audience that, near the end of the play, the Friar quite literally finds himself running from the carnage he helped to bring about, only to stumble into the Prince's coterie. [*AO1 for advancing the argument with a judiciously selected quote; AO2 for observing how form shapes meaning*].

- Despite trying to offer sound guidance, the Friar confusingly allows himself to go along with this mad and arguably childish plan to marry the lovers – 'I'll thy assistant be' – and, as a result, he becomes an accessory to the "crime."

- *Elsewhere in the play*: The pain caused by hastily agreeing to marry the young lovers not only impacts on the parents, but also on others who love and care for the young lovers. The Nurse is a case in point: a character who has lost her own offspring and who considers Juliet as something of a surrogate child.

Conclusion

As it so happens, I have another theme up my sleeve about the Friar's ability to empathise; however, I believe that the first three themes are more than enough to fill the time one would have in the exam. As a result, I would be tempted to condense my final theme into a kind of afterthought that enlivens the conclusion...

"The Friar – like many characters in the play – defies easy categorisation: the more one scratches the surface, the more the complexities abound. This extract, for instance, presents him as truly empathetic of the lovers: when he proclaims 'I'll thy assistant be,' he is doing the lovers the courtesy of respecting and acting on their emotions (in stark contrast to Capulet, who slaps down

Juliet's feelings). However, one could just as easily argue that he proves not empathetic enough: he is more concerned with simply healing the feud than for the lovers themselves. The audience is left with the mindset of a 'waverer:' unable to make a definitive verdict on the Friar either way."

A statue of Shakespeare in Stratford-upon-Avon, the town in which he was born

At this point in the play, Mercutio has just been stabbed by Tybalt and has sustained a mortal wound.

MERCUTIO
I am hurt.
A plague o' both your houses! I am sped.
Is he gone, and hath nothing?
BENVOLIO
What, art thou hurt?
MERCUTIO
Ay, ay, a scratch, a scratch; marry, 'tis enough.
Where is my page? Go, villain, fetch a surgeon.
Exit Page
ROMEO
Courage, man; the hurt cannot be much.
MERCUTIO
No, 'tis not so deep as a well, nor so wide as a

church-door; but 'tis enough, 'twill serve: ask for
me to-morrow, and you shall find me a grave man. I
am peppered, I warrant, for this world. A plague o'
both your houses! 'Zounds, a dog, a rat, a mouse, a
cat, to scratch a man to death! a braggart, a
rogue, a villain, that fights by the book of
arithmetic! Why the devil came you between us? I
was hurt under your arm.

**Starting with this exchange, explain how far
you think Shakespeare presents Mercutio as
a heroic character.**

Write about:

**• how Shakespeare presents Mercutio in this
extract.**

**• how Shakespeare presents Mercutio in the
play as a whole.**

Introduction

As ever, my first sentence scores AO3, contextual marks; and
my second sentence broaches the AO1 ideas the essay will
explore.

"Although the characters Romeo and Juliet kick against
the Classical pricks – in Greek tragedies, the heroes
were always of royal birth – Mercutio, to the extent he
can be considered a hero, more closely abides by the

Classical formula: he is the Prince's cousin.[1] However, while Mercutio is heroic in many respects – he is knocked down in the prime of life; he is fatally flawed by his exuberant arrogance – there are also aspects that undercut his heroic status, chief among them his desperate attempts to cast himself as the hero."

Theme/Paragraph One: Mercutio is a heroic character due to his capacity for self-sacrifice: he places himself in mortal peril to protect Romeo, then attempts to shield Romeo from the severity of his injuries.

- This entire scene comes about because Mercutio courageously intervenes to protect his friend, Romeo. As a result, the fatal wound Mercutio sustains in this extract is the fallout from an act of heroism.
- Mercutio's strange, understated assessment of his wound arguably redoubles his heroism, since it can very easily be construed as an effort by Mercutio to protect Romeo from the *emotional* pain he understands this injury will cause: Mercutio dismisses the wound as 'a scratch, a scratch.' The strain of putting on a brave face is revealed as Mercutio reiterates this assessment: 'No, 'tis not so deep as a well.' That the line starts with three inverted trochaic feet reveals his true pain: his speech pattern has been thrown for a loop. [*AO1 for advancing the argument with a judiciously selected quote; AO2 for the close analysis of the language*].

- Although Mercutio does indeed sacrifice himself for Romeo, the heroism is, however, undercut by Mercutio's resentment at being compelled to act heroically. The exclamation 'A plague o' both your houses' is telling. One might even contend that the plague that later stops Friar John from delivering a crucial message to Romeo, and leads to the final double-suicide, is a *direct result* of Mercutio's curse – rendering it an act of revenge that cancels out Mercutio's act of heroism.

Theme/Paragraph Two: Mercutio's arrogance and rashness is a character flaw that in some senses elevates him to a tragic hero, and yet, in others, arguably makes him a kind of anti-hero.

- Mercutio, throughout the play, behaves impulsively and with a self-assurance that borders on reckless arrogance. The fact Mercutio engages Tybalt at all exemplifies this. Although Mercutio mocks Tybalt as fighting 'by the book of arithmetic,' Tybalt is earlier portrayed as a fearsome fighter. The way Mercutio reprimands Romeo near the end of this extract – 'Why the devil came you between us?' – exposes the sheer lack of foresight to his action: his rash plan had not taken into account this possibility. [*AO1 for advancing the argument with a judiciously selected quote*].
- Aristotle, a seminal Greek philosopher, argued that the key marker of a tragic hero was a fatal character flaw that leads to their downfall (known as a

hamartia).[2] Since Aristotle was widely read in Elizabethan England, Shakespeare's audience would have been alert to the fact that Mercutio's rashness marked him out as a tragic hero. One might also note that it was Mercutio's rashness and arrogance in leading the Montagues to the Capulets' party (and thus provoking Tybalt) that brought about this altercation in the first place. [*AO3 for placing the play in a cultural, literary, and historical context*].

- It should be observed, however, that a modern audience – trained to conceive of a hero as noble and virtuous – may believe these character flaws in fact negate Mercutio's heroic status.

Theme/Paragraph Three: Mercutio self-consciously casts himself as a hero, which ironically serves to undermine his heroic status.

- Even though Mercutio is dying, he is still putting on a performance in which he has self-consciously cast himself as the hero. Tellingly, he first calls his Page a 'villain,' and then describes Tybalt as 'a / rogue, a villain:' the implication is that Mercutio, by contrast, is the hero of the story. Moreover, he attempts to deploy humour to lend a leading-man charisma to his dying words. Particularly striking is the wordplay in his quip: 'ask for me tomorrow and you shall find me a grave man' – 'grave' both referring to his state of mind and the fact he shall physically be in a grave. However, the humour falls flat: he comes across as a pretender, desperately trying to conjure the memorable last words he feels befit a hero. [*AO1 for advancing the argument with a judiciously selected quote; AO2 for the close analysis of the language*].

- *Elsewhere in the play*: At other points in the play, when Mercutio places himself centre stage less heavy-handedly, it functions to truly elevate him to hero status: the Queen Mab speech, for instance, is a master class in poetic lyricism that steals the show: indeed, it is placed just before the Capulet's party, which, structurally speaking, renders it a kind of dramatic prologue to the festivities. However, in *this* extract, his attempt is self-defeating: he is a man emulating a hero, *not* the real deal. [*AO2 for observing how structure shapes meaning*].

Conclusion

On this occasion, I am yet again planning to slip an extra argument into the conclusion: namely, a conversation of how the timing of Mercutio's death impacts on his heroic status (an attempt not only to score extra AO1 marks, but which also hopes to score AO2 for commentary on structure). You will notice as well that I also bring in the text from which Shakespeare pinched his storyline for *Romeo and Juliet*, thereby also scoring an AO3 point or two!

"Whether Mercutio's performance 'tis enough' to earn hero status seems to have been left by Shakespeare intentionally ambiguous. The structure of the play seems to undercut his heroic status: he does not even appear in the second half. Yet, the fact that in Shakespeare's source material (Arthur Brooke's *Romeus and Juliet*, 1562) Mercutio does not exist, seems to suggest the opposite: that Shakespeare invented Mercutio purposively to plug a vacuum. Mercutio, therefore, is the self-dramatising hero, ever aggrieved about the leading-man, Romeo, stepping between him and the audience: 'Why the devil came you between us?'"

Shakespeare inspired street art (I somehow feel as though Mercutio would have appreciated it!)

READ THE FOLLOWING EXTRACT FROM
ACT 3 SCENE 1 OF ROMEO AND JULIET
AND THEN ANSWER THE QUESTION THAT
FOLLOWS.

At this point in the play, Romeo has just killed Tybalt and various individuals have arrived at the scene.

LADY CAPULET

I beg for justice, which thou, prince, must give;
Romeo slew Tybalt, Romeo must not live.

PRINCE

Romeo slew him, he slew Mercutio;
Who now the price of his dear blood doth owe?

MONTAGUE

Not Romeo, prince, he was Mercutio's friend;
His fault concludes but what the law should end,
The life of Tybalt.

PRINCE

And for that offence
Immediately we do exile him hence:
I have an interest in your hate's proceeding,

My blood for your rude brawls doth lie a-bleeding;
But I'll amerce you with so strong a fine
That you shall all repent the loss of mine:
I will be deaf to pleading and excuses;
Nor tears nor prayers shall purchase out abuses:
Therefore use none: let Romeo hence in haste,
Else, when he's found, that hour is his last.
Bear hence this body and attend our will:
Mercy but murders, pardoning those that kill.

Starting with this exchange, explain how Shakespeare presents the idea of justice in *Romeo and Juliet*.

Write about:

- **how Shakespeare presents the idea of justice in this extract.**

- **how Shakespeare presents the idea of justice in the play as a whole.**

Introduction

"Elizabethan England was not only a place preoccupied with justice, but also one in which individuals routinely took justice into their own hands; indeed, given that the playwrights Ben Jonson and Christopher Marlowe were both separately involved in duels, Elizabethans would have been unflustered by the idea of Mercutio dying in a fight. Shakespeare, through Lady Capulet and Montague, explores two different conceptions of justice: revenge and vigilantism. However, while the Prince also contemplates justice, he is chiefly used as a vehicle to convey the fallibility of those charged with executing justice."

Theme/Paragraph One: Justice is compromised by the fallibility of the humans in power: the Prince is unable to make an impartial decision because Mercutio is his cousin.

- That the Prince is personally invested in Mercutio – his cousin – perverts his ability to effectively dish out impartial justice. As a result, justice is distorted by the whims of a powerful yet fallible human being. The Prince makes his lack of partiality explicit with the blunt observation that 'I have an interest in your hate's proceedings:' his 'interest' is not simply the fact that this is his town, but the fact the casualty is his cousin. [*AO1 for advancing the argument with a judiciously selected quote; AO2 for the close analysis of the language*].
- The Prince emphasises how profoundly invested he is in Mercutio by stating that the spilling of Mercutio's blood is synonymous with the spilling of his own: 'My blood for your rude brawls doth lie a-bleeding.' One might observe that the unstressed hyperbeat at the end of this quote causes the line to overrun the iambic pentameter, almost as though reflecting Mercutio's

(and, by extension, the Prince's) blood spilling over. Given the Prince's deep emotional investment in the spilling of royal blood, Shakespeare casts serious doubts on the Prince's ability to dole out impartial justice: he makes clear that he intends to make the warring houses 'repent the loss of mine.' [AO2 *for the close analysis of the language*].

- *Elsewhere in the play*: The theme of miscarriages of justice due to human imperfection appears at other points in the play as well. For instance, Romeo kills Paris; however, this killing does not seem just; instead, it appears to flow from Romeo's out-of-control passion.

Theme/Paragraph Two: Shakespeare uses Lady Capulet here as the mouthpiece for an 'eye-for-an-eye' philosophy of justice: Lady Capulet sees justice as the counterbalancing of a crime with an equal and opposite action.

- Throughout the play, both the Montagues and the Capulets take a largely "eye-for-an-eye" view of justice: they see it as transactional – the taking of a life can only be adequately counterbalanced by the taking of another, regardless of the circumstances. The way Lady Capulet incurs an intimate chain of logic when discussing Romeo and Tybalt – 'Romeo slew Tybalt' ergo 'Romeo must not live' – reveals her deeply transactional view of justice: just as the names act as counterbalances in the sentence, so too must their lives counterbalance one another. Moreover, her assertion that 'I beg for justice' seeks to cast justice as something akin to currency: something that you can 'beg' for, and which can then be used to settle debt. [*AO1 for advancing the argument with a judiciously selected quote; AO2 for the close analysis of the language*].

- The Prince also partially buys into this 'eye-for-an-eye' mentality: he sees the murder of his cousin, Mercutio, as the accruing of a debt, or 'fine,' that must be paid off in order for justice to prevail, and which is too great to be settled ('purchase[d] out') with 'tears and prayers.'

- *Elsewhere in the play*: The very start of the play introduces the idea of transactional justice. The Montagues and Capulets are working out which party has bitten their thumb at the other, so they can return the favour.

Theme/Paragraph Three: Shakespeare, through Montague's comments, outlines a different conception of justice – namely, vigilantism: the notion that breaking the law is acceptable when it is to uphold the law.

- Shakespeare introduces the idea of vigilantism in this extract: the idea that breaking the law is permissible when done to uphold the law. Indeed, this is the argument that Montague puts forward in Romeo's defence when he states that Romeo's 'fault concludes but what the law should end, / The life of Tybalt.' Montague here is observing that, if Tybalt was still alive, the law would be compelled to punish him with death for his murder of Mercutio. In doing so, Montague implicitly equates Romeo with the law, casting his actions as an embodiment of justice, not crime. The short phrase, 'the life of Tybalt,' constitutes a standalone line, and creates a sense of finality, thereby causing the form to neatly mirror the finality implied by Montague's logic. [*AO1 for advancing the argument with a judiciously selected quote; AO2 for observing how form shapes meaning*].

- *Elsewhere in the play*: Shakespeare explores vigilantism at other points in the play – indeed, Mercutio – just prior to this extract – has himself played vigilante: when he fights Tybalt, he is breaking the law in order to defy someone who is threatening to break the law.

Theme/Paragraph Four: Shakespeare in this passage points to a shocking absence of divine justice in these proceedings: the Prince rebukes the concept of prayers.

- The religious language in this passage – more precisely, the Prince's comment that neither 'tears nor prayers shall purchase out abuses' – draws attention to the notion of divine justice. While on one level one might simply glean that the Prince is saying that words alone cannot compensate for Mercutio's death, he may also be suggesting that divine powers cannot be depended on to deliver justice. Indeed, by this point in the play, is certainly seems as though the Prince is justified to feel this way: the play's chaos brings to mind Gloucester's words in King Lear: 'As flies to wanton boys, are we to the gods. / They kill us for their sport.' [*AO3 for invoking a second text that deepens our understanding*].

- However, one might argue that divine justice does ultimately prevail. Mercutio, as he dies, curses the lovers: 'A plague o' both your houses.' Sure enough, as if by divine intervention, the plague later stops Friar John delivering a crucial message to Romeo and thus precipitates Romeo's death. Elizabethans understood the bubonic plague as a punishment from God – something akin to the plagues that blighted Egypt in the Old Testament. As a result, these events would certainly have been construed as divine justice by Shakespeare's audience. [*AO1 for advancing the argument with a judiciously selected quote; AO3 for commentary on the beliefs and goings-on of the Elizabethan period*].

Conclusion

Because this plan has not yet commented meaningfully on structure, an often overlooked dimension of AO2, this is going to be a key ingredient in my conclusion. I shall then wrap things up with a nod back to the essay question.

"One might note that the structure of this extract seems to constitute a Hegelian dialectic: Lady Capulet presents a thesis in favour of tit-for-tat justice; Montague presents an antithesis in favour of vigilantism; and the Prince's speech becomes a kind of synthesis.[1] This seems to embody Shakespeare's technique in *Romeo and Juliet* (and, indeed, all his plays). Shakespeare's texts revel in exploring the philosophical underpinnings to concepts such as justice, while concealing its author's views. One comes away with the impression that the ambiguity of justice is perhaps its most important quality in Shakespeare's estimation."

READ THE FOLLOWING EXTRACT FROM
ACT 3 SCENE 5 OF ROMEO AND JULIET
AND THEN ANSWER THE QUESTION THAT
FOLLOWS.

A t this point in the play, Romeo has been banished from Verona for killing Tybalt, and Juliet is under pressure to marry Paris.

JULIET
What say'st thou? hast thou not a word of joy?
Some comfort, nurse.
NURSE
Faith, here it is.
Romeo is banish'd; and all the world to nothing,
That he dares ne'er come back to challenge you;
Or, if he do, it needs must be by stealth.
Then, since the case so stands as now it doth,
I think it best you married with the county.
O, he's a lovely gentleman!
Romeo's a dishclout to him: an eagle, madam,
Hath not so green, so quick, so fair an eye
As Paris hath. Beshrew my very heart,
I think you are happy in this second match,

For it excels your first: or if it did not,
Your first is dead; or 'twere as good he were,
As living here and you no use of him.
JULIET
Speakest thou from thy heart?

Starting with this conversation, discuss to what extent the Nurse is portrayed as a maternal figure in the play?

Write about:

• **how Shakespeare presents the Nurse in this extract.**

• **how Shakespeare presents the Nurse in the play as a whole.**

Introduction

The same old formula: I am starting with an AO3 titbit of context, then following up with some indication of the themes I'm planning to throw down.

"Given that the Elizabethan era was blighted by eye-watering infant mortality rates, it is little surprise that the Nurse – who early on in the play reveals that she lost her daughter, Susan – latches onto Juliet as a surrogate daughter. However, while the Nurse exhibits a number of deeply maternal instincts (a common-sense pragmatism, a capacity for empathy), there are crucial times where these instincts fall short."

Theme/Paragraph One: The Nurse exercises a kind of maternal pragmatism in this extract: she reasons that, since Romeo is no longer a viable option, Juliet's interests would be best served by coupling up with Paris.

- The Nurse in this passage is being eminently pragmatic, which is arguably a deeply maternal trait. The Nurse traces the logic in plain language: she first observes that 'Romeo is banish'd,' then states simply 'since the case so stands... / I think it best you married with the county.' The word 'case' lends her language a legalese quality; and the unstressed hyperbeat created by the word 'county' requires the iambic pentameter to compromise in a way that mirrors the compromise the Nurse is suggesting.[1] Although she is not counselling Juliet to follow her heart, she is arguably using logic to look out for her best interests. [*AO1 for advancing the argument with a judiciously selected quote; AO2 for the close analysis of the language*].

- Maternal pragmatism, however, ought to be joined with emotional support, and the Nurse does little to console her about the loss of Romeo: the bluntness of 'Your first is dead' is striking.

- *Elsewhere in the play*: Moreover, one might observe, though, that the Nurse's maternal pragmatism here is anomalous: her primary mode is usually far more emotive and humour-based. The Nurse that exchanges jocularities with Mercutio in Act 2 seems worlds away from this logical creature.

Theme/Paragraph Two: Although the Nurse fails to console Juliet about the loss of Romeo, she attempts to comfort Juliet by singing Paris's praises and trying to get her to see a silver lining.

- The Nurse is arguably trying to comfort Juliet by choosing not to force Paris on her, but rather to try and sell his best attributes and how these attributes allow him to outshine Romeo. She asserts that 'He's a lovely gentleman,' and draws attention to his good looks: 'so green, so quick, so fair an eye / As Paris hath.' The repetition of 'so' is a simple yet effective tactic to add emphasis to her praise. [*AO1 for advancing the argument with a judiciously selected quote; AO2 for the close analysis of the language*].
- Although this may reveal an ignorance of Juliet's intense feelings towards Romeo, it does demonstrate a maternal empathy for Juliet: the Nurse sincerely wants her to like Paris and be happy with the match. This stands in contrast to Capulet, who does not appear to care about Juliet's feelings towards Paris.
- While the Nurse's efforts here seems sincere, the language she uses to praise Paris seems to fall slightly short: her assertion that 'Romeo's a dishclout to him' feels a pale imitation of Hamlet's assessment of how his usurping uncle fails to measure up to his father: 'Hyperion to a satyr.'[2] [*AO3 for invoking another text that allows us to place this one in context*].

Theme/Paragraph Three: The Nurse's attempt to throw her weight behind Paris could be construed as a type of maternal discipline: she is attempting to draw boundaries.

- Arguably, the Nurse is also appearing as a disciplinarian in this extract. She does not take Juliet's side; she joins her parents in counselling her to jettison Romeo and opt for Paris. If one looks again at her words – 'I think it best you married with the county' – it is not difficult to see the phrase 'it best' as a muffled imperative, a euphemism that sublimates a direct command.[3] [*AO1 for advancing the argument with a judiciously selected quote; AO2 for the close analysis of the language*].

- *Elsewhere in the play:* While the Nurse may stake claim to a maternal disciplinarian mantle here, it is easy to see it as too little and too late to be drawing boundaries. Indeed, it is because she failed to give Juliet boundaries earlier, and in fact assisted her in her courtship with Romeo, that Juliet has wound up in this position in the first place. That this scene immediately precedes one in which Juliet and Friar Laurence hatch their dangerous plan to stage her death places structural emphasis on the Nurse's prior failures that might have averted this scenario. [*AO2 for discussing how structure shapes meaning*].

- Moreover, one may see this extract not as a virtuous attempt at drawing boundaries, but instead as an abdication of her maternal responsibilities by towing Capulet's line and is arguably just cynically trying to keep on side of her employers. However, given the pressure on women in Elizabethan society to submit to the patriarch's will, this may be understandable. [*AO3 for invoking historical context that deepens our understanding of the text*].

Theme/Paragraph Four: Although she is telling Juliet to give up on Romeo, she inadvertently posits a scenario in which Romeo could conceivably return, perhaps revealing an unconscious maternal desire to see Juliet's wish fulfilled.

- The Nurse demonstrates herself to be unconsciously divided: although she is telling Juliet to give up on Romeo, she inadvertently reveals a secret sadness and regret for Juliet when she briefly posits a scenario in which he could conceivably return: 'Or, if he do, it needs must be by stealth.' Even though saying this is not particularly useful in helping Juliet to overcome her sadness, this Freudian slip shows that unconsciously she wants Juliet to have the relationship she most desires – which is arguably a very maternal instinct.[4] Indeed, this tallies with the Nurse's prior actions in brokering the extemporary marriage, and playing intermediary. [*AO1 for advancing the argument with a judiciously selected quote*].

- While the Nurse is unintentionally creating false hope in Juliet by presenting this eventuality in which she could be with Romeo, it still reveals a deeply maternal instinct: she is feeling Juliet's pain and very personally. The internal half-rhyme on 'needs' and 'be' creates a secret subtext in which the Nurse seems to hint at her understanding that Juliet's 'need' for Romeo is an existential one (without him, she cannot 'be'). [*AO2 for the close analysis of the language*].

Conclusion

Although I invoke another Shakespeare play here in a nod to AO3 (*A Midsummer's Night Dream*), and I make a brief mention of form impacting on meaning (AO2), the focus in this conclusion – given that I've already covered all the themes I was hoping to – is to succinctly tie up the arguments.

"After Juliet's drugged body is discovered in Act 4, the Nurse's lamentations encapsulate her status as a well-meaning-yet-inadequate maternal figure. They seem at once sincere (an attempt to 'speakest... from [her] heart,' taking the form of an iambic pentameter that lends it superficial formality), yet also so histrionic that the Nurse unintentionally strikes an absurd figure – more Midsummer rude mechanical than reposed matriarch.[5] Ultimately, while the Nurse genuinely attempts to cast herself as a caring maternal figure, she falls short due to inadequacies in her character; for instance, the lack of judgement that led her to facilitate the marriage in the first place."

READ THE FOLLOWING EXTRACT FROM
ACT 5 SCENE 3 OF ROMEO AND JULIET
AND THEN ANSWER THE QUESTION THAT
FOLLOWS.

At this point in the play, Romeo and Juliet have both died, and the Prince, Capulet and Montague – among others – have arrived at the crypt.

PRINCE
And here he writes that he did buy a poison
Of a poor 'pothecary, and therewithal
Came to this vault to die, and lie with Juliet.
Where be these enemies? Capulet! Montague!
See, what a scourge is laid upon your hate,
That heaven finds means to kill your joys with love.
And I for winking at your discords too
Have lost a brace of kinsmen: all are punish'd.
CAPULET
O brother Montague, give me thy hand:
This is my daughter's jointure, for no more
Can I demand.
MONTAGUE

But I can give thee more:
For I will raise her statue in pure gold;
That while Verona by that name is known,
There shall no figure at such rate be set
As that of true and faithful Juliet.

Starting with this conversation, explain how Shakespeare portrays grief in *Romeo and Juliet*.

Write about:

• **how Shakespeare portray grief in this extract.**

• **how Shakespeare portray grief in the play as a whole.**

Introduction

"Grief was at the heart of Elizabethan England, a country living in the wake of the devastating bubonic plague: the very same plague that precipitates tragedy in the play by preventing Friar John from delivering a crucial missive to Romeo. While the Nurse's reaction to Juliet's supposed death earlier in the play arguably strikes an absurd, even comical tone, Shakespeare's dealings with grief tends largely to be sombre-minded, portraying it as an emotion that dulls hatreds and even inspires artistic creation."

Theme/Paragraph One: Grief is portrayed as a tonic that dulls both Capulet's and Montague's urge to fight and, as a result, leads to an uneasy peace.

- Capulet and Montague are placed in the unusual situation of experiencing a symmetrical trauma: they have both lost a child. As a result, their instinct to argue is displaced by an urge to make amends. 'O brother Montague, give me thy hand,' is striking language: Sampson's insulting nickname in the play's opening scene for the opposing house – 'a dog from the house of Montague' – has been switched for the epithet 'brother.' That such different language characterises the play's opening and closing sequences adds structural emphasis to the transformation. [*AO1 for advancing the argument with a judiciously selected quote; AO2 for the close analysis of the language*].

- The metre itself is made to mimic the newfound accord between Capulet and Montague: Capulet's final words in this extract, 'Can I demand,' crucially start a fresh line of verse, and are followed by Montague finishing the iambic pentameter: 'But I can give thee more.' Only when their words combine do we have the five metrical feet, thereby causing the form reflect the newfound synthesis between them. [*AO2 for discussing how structure shapes meaning*].

- *Elsewhere in the play*: Elsewhere in the play, the grief induced is unable to inspire such a détente; indeed, the grief after the death of Tybalt, for instance, seems to only fan the flames of the Capulets' anger. It is only a mutual, deep grief that cuts through the noise.

Theme/Paragraph Two: Grief is portrayed as an animating force that inspires artistic creation.

- The Prince reflects that the death of Romeo and Juliet represents the demise of Montague's and Capulet's respective 'joy.' In response to this loss, both Montague and Capulet air their emotions in a way that comes across as strikingly and self-consciously poetic. Capulet's brief three lines are lyrical, with a striking rhyme between 'demand' and 'hand' that draws attention to the intentional poetry. This is accentuated by the finely-balanced metre of the line 'This is my daughter's jointure, for no more,' because although the line contains trochaic words – 'daughter's,' 'jointure' – Capulet maintains consistent iambic metre throughout.[1] [*AO1 for advancing the argument with a judiciously selected quote; AO2 for the close analysis of the language*].

- Not only does Montague's response, with its rhyming couplet of 'set' and 'Juliet,' constitute a similar kind of poetry, but he explicitly asserts his intention to create a statue – another form of artistry – to honour his former rival's daughter: 'I will raise [Juliet's] statue in pure gold.' However, one might note that the invocation of 'gold' comes across as almost gauche, and is reminiscent of the golden cow that appears as a false idol in the Old Testament.[2] Shakespeare could be implying that this particular proposed act of artistry is wrongheaded, and may reflect a sense among Protestants in England that their Catholic counterparts in Italy practised an immoral version of Christianity. [*AO3 for placing the play in historical/cultural context*].

- *Elsewhere in the play*: One might note that poetic set-pieces also appear in the sequence after Juliet's (supposedly) dead body is found in her bed. On that occasion, too, Capulet launches into poetic lamentation.

Theme/Paragraph Three: While grief is portrayed as an emotion that inspires poetry, and even peace, one might note that, throughout the play, grief is often portrayed in the precise opposite fashion: as an emotion that begets further loss and grief.

- As the Prince chastises Montague and Capulet at the start of this extract, he reflects on the loss he has sustained during the course of the play: 'I for winking at your discords too / Have lost a brace of kinsmen.' The kinsman that he has most noticeably lost is his cousin, Mercutio. One might note that it is in no small part Romeo's grief at the death of Mercutio, however, that eggs him into taking Tybalt's life. This, in turn, not only sparks a fresh round of grief among the Capulets at the death of Tybalt, but also induces grief in Juliet at the exile of Romeo. [*AO1 for advancing the argument with a judiciously selected quote*].
- When the Prince notes that 'All are punish'd,' he is observing that the warring houses have been punished precisely for their shared determination to ensure that grief-inducing acts committed against them are always avenged by grief-inspiring violence. (Indeed, the lost 'e' caused by the elision in 'punish'd' might reflect the endless lost lives that inspire grief through the play).

Grief, therefore, is portrayed as an emotion that spawns more grief, and as a weapon that both houses have deployed against the other – the emotional equivalent of 'poison / Of a poor 'pothecary.'

Conclusion

I have a final point I want to cover in the conclusion – namely, that grief has caused an erosion in the Prince's faith in civil society. However, aside from this extra attempt to score AO1 marks, you will notice a nod to Shakespeare's *King Lear*, in a final gambit to pick up AO3 marks potentially going spare.

"As the Prince harangues the Montagues and Capulets, it is evident that something else has been lost as a result of the Prince's grief: his faith in civic society. Throughout the play, the Prince, through his attempts to intervene, has exhibited an implicit hope that relations between the houses might improve. However, his nihilistic words here – 'see, what a scourge is laid upon your hate' – suggests that grief has caused this to wither as well, thereby ensuring that grief is portrayed as something that degrades as much as heals. One is reminded of the loss in faith in humanity and existence itself that Lear experiences after the death of his daughter, Cordelia."

A statue of Juliet in Verona, Italy.

ENDNOTES

ESSAY PLAN ONE

1. To be ambivalent is to have mixed feelings about something or someone.
2. If something has been marred, it has been damaged or disfigured.
3. If someone is mercurial, it means their mood or state of mind is frequently subject to change.
4. Elision is when you remove a syllable or a sound from a word, and is usually signified by an apostrophe replacing the missing syllable. We use elision all the time in present-day English – for example, 'let's' and 'I'm'.
5. A *volte-face* is when someone takes the polar opposite view to the one they previously held.
6. An elegy is a lyric or poem that involves deep contemplation, and is most frequently seen during the commemoration of a death.
7. A provocateur is someone who intentionally acts in such a way as to provoke strong emotions in others.

ESSAY PLAN TWO

1. I suspect you are asking: what is an inverted trochaic foot? Let me explain from the top.

    Shakespeare's plays are almost entirely written in *iambic pentameter*. An iamb is a metrical foot in which the emphasis is on the second syllable, and tends to sound more like natural speech. A pentameter is when there are five metrical feet in a line.

    It is often easiest to illustrate with an example. If we take the first line of Romeo's response to the servant, and use bold font to represent the stressed syllables, plus a vertical bar to indicate the end of each metrical foot, it will look like this: 'O, **she** | doth **teach** | the **torch** | es **to** | burn **bright**.' Since there are five metrical feet here, all iambic, it is rendered in iambic pentameter.

    A trochee, on the other hand, is a metrical foot in which the emphasis is on the first syllable, and tends to sound more unnatural. To illustrate, let's look at the penultimate line from this extract, and mark out the stresses on syllables: '**Did** my | **heart** love | **till** now? | for**swear** | it, **sight**!' As you can see, the first three metrical feet are trochees, which is unusual for Shakespeare. In fact, it is precisely because Shakespeare does not usually use trochees that we call these *inverted* trochaic feet: he is inverting how he usually does things.

ESSAY PLAN THREE

1. If something is didactic, it seeks to impart a moral lesson.

ESSAY PLAN FOUR

1. To kick against the pricks is to resist the way something is done, often in a way that ends up hurting oneself.
2. This idea is introduced in Aristotle's *Poetics*, in which he outlines the nature of tragedy.

ESSAY PLAN FIVE

1. G. W. F. Hegel was a Nineteenth Century German Philosopher, and his style of argumentation often took the form described above: first came the thesis – a kind of initial argument; then the antithesis – an opposing argument; then, finally, a synthesis, which finds a way to resolve the tension between the thesis and the antithesis.

ESSAY PLAN SIX

1. An unstressed hyperbeat is when there is an extra, unstressed syllable going spare.
   If we take the line under discussion, and mark out the metre, it would look as follows: 'I **think** | it **best** | you **marr** | ied **with** | the **coun** | ty.' As you can see, there are five consecutive iambs, then one extra, unstressed syllable going spare. This is the unstressed hyperbeat – though it used to be referred to as a "feminine ending."
   As an aside, when you have a stressed extra syllable, it is called a stressed hyperbeat (and, formerly, a "masculine ending").
2. Shakespeare's *Hamlet* revolves around Hamlet's efforts to take revenge against Claudius, because Claudius (Hamlet's uncle) has secretly killed Hamlet's father (and the former King) in order to steal the throne.
   In Greek myth, Hyperion is the Titan god of light, whereas a satyr is a man-goat hybrid.
3. A euphemism is when you say something in a roundabout and less direct way
4. A Freudian slip is when you accidentally say something, or misspeak, in a way that reveals your true intentions or thoughts. It is an allusion to the father of psychoanalysis, Sigmund Freud (1856 – 1939).
5. In *A Midsummer Night's Dream*, a group of labourers, known as the

mechanicals, put on a play for the Duke, and they are comedically portrayed as unintentionally absurd.

ESSAY PLAN SEVEN

1. A line can be rendered in perfect iambic pentameter, but contain words that are, in isolation, trochaic. It does so by breaking the trochaic words across two metrical feet. This creates a strange tension, because whereas the iambic feet create a rising rhythm, the trochaic words create a falling one.

2. At one point in the Old Testament, Moses climbs up Mount Sinai to receive the ten commandments from God, but returns to find the children of Israel worshipping a false idol – namely, a gold cow.

AFTERWORD

To keep up to date with Accolade Press, visit https://accoladetuition.com/accolade-press. You can also join our private Facebook group (where our authors share resources and guidance) by visiting the following link: https://rcl.ink/DME.

Also, if you found this edition useful, we'd hugely appreciate a review on Amazon. You can leave your feedback by heading here: https://rcl.ink/DMN.